When Police Officers Stand Down

The Effects of Depolicing in America

A Police Officer's Point of View

I0416966

Michael H. Schmitz

Table of Contents

Introduction

In recent years, cities across America have experienced some of the largest and most expensive citizen uprisings in recent history. Today's police are feeling the restrain of being questioned for their actions, whether or not they are justified. There is one big factor that the citizens need to be aware of: depolicing.

Depolicing is a term that is somewhat new to social conversations within the United States. It is a phenomenon that has gripped communities recently and will have drastic consequences once it takes hold across America.

I have been in law enforcement for the past 20 years. Not all of that time has been spent as a street cop; some of that time has been spent in many other forms of law enforcement. As a small child growing up in the Midwest, I was always the one that had to play the "cop" when playing "cops and robbers" with my friends. During my high school years, I, like so many other teenagers, took a career assessment exam to see which field I would be most likely to work in. As predicted, my exam returned with law enforcement being at the top. At this time in my life, law enforcement was the furthest from my mind. I had lost interest in my childhood role as "cop".

Upon graduating high school, my interest in a career in law enforcement returned, and I attended a local technical college pursuing an associate's degree in police science. I was still uncertain if this was something I wanted to do as a career but continued my education, nonetheless.

After graduating college, I began the testing process with various departments in my local area. I took a job as a security officer at a local inner city mall and worked closely with law enforcement. After all, we had a police substation inside of the mall, and I worked with the same police officers daily.

During my early years, I was always drawn to helping others. As a teenager in high school, I worked as a life guard and swim instructor and enjoyed teaching the younger kids and keeping guard while they swam during open swimming sessions.

Having served for several years as a patrol officer in a diverse community and having watched the career that I dreamed about for most of my life being scrutinized, I feel it is now time to give the perspective of someone who is on the street day in, day out. Although it bothers me to see my brothers and sisters being put on the chopping block, I understand that, at times, there are officers that may not have people's best interest at heart. But the percentage of those officers is so small that it is hardly worth targeting.

To understand police use of force, you must understand one key point: when a police officer uses force to affect an arrest or stop a crime from happening, it is always a "shock and awe" response. Police officers are trained to "stop the threat or action" IMMEDIATELY. In several incidents this is not possible. As more and more people resist police or are non-compliant, officers will increase their level of force. Keep in mind that police officers will use more force than the force used against them to reach the goal of stopping the threat or action of another. It just makes sense. Otherwise, you will see a tug-of-war match between offenders and police that could go on for several minutes. The longer these incidents take to resolve, the greater the risk of injury to the officer and the citizen.

Police use of force has been scrutinized for decades. Departments across the country are continually trying to find ways to stop an offender that are less injurious to the offender yet strong enough to bring the confrontation to a quick conclusion. This is a daunting task, as technology is not perfect. Each year, a new tool is marketed to law enforcement agencies that is supposed to be more effective and less lethal than prior years'.

This brings us to where our country is today. I am not going to discuss the race issue that has been spreading throughout media outlets across the country. Everyone has a different opinion on this issue, and no one has a direct resolution, as far as I have seen.

Chapter 1: Police Mindset

I can honestly say that the majority—a large majority—of police officers across this country have the same goal: to protect those who cannot protect themselves. Protecting property falls somewhere towards the bottom of the priority list. Police officers are willing, without a second thought, to run into danger to protect those they serve from harm. But this doesn't happen very often. But when it does, those officers will respond without forethought.

So, you ask yourself, "What goes through a police officer's mind during these critical responses?" I can't answer this for anyone else. But the first thing that goes through my mind are my wife and child. As I turn on my emergency lights and siren, I quietly tell my wife and child that I love them. As I get closer to the incident, I wonder where the aggressor is, what's in their hands, and what they are doing. As I get out of my patrol vehicle, I think tactics. Where is my cover? If they do this then I'll do that. All of these thoughts go through your mind within seconds. That's all the time you have to identify the threat and devise a plan. These situations develop in mere seconds.

As an officer, you have to make life and death decisions in split seconds. Most police shootings take place in less than 6 seconds. You better have your plan in place or you'll be in serious trouble. The one thing that has recently caused officers to be hesitant—which can be deadly—is wondering what will happen after the incident has ended. So, within seconds, you need to identify the threat, have a plan, and execute your plan. If an officer is concerned about the ramifications of their actions, regardless of whether or not they are justified, that takes about 3 seconds off the clock. By this time you are in what officers call code black. This is a very dangerous place to be. You are in panic mode, and nothing will go right!

In the past, police officers didn't worry about the ramifications of their actions. They knew they needed to get to the scene and help someone, not worry about helping themselves. Unfortunately, this mindset has begun to diminish, quickly. Officers will slow down their actions. Some may even stop a block away from the incident and think about whether or not it's worth it to respond quickly. When this happens, citizens get hurt—or even killed.

Officers used to put their families second to those they serve. This is what has made law enforcement one of the most respected careers in history. This is also one of the main reasons why police officers have such a high divorce rate. Police officers relive critical incidents for many weeks after the incident has ended. They bring it home. They cry in the dark and place a great burden on themselves for the incidents they respond to. Police officers want to save everyone. They feel responsible for those they weren't able to help—even when the citizenhas placed themselves in the situation. Police want to help.

Chapter 2: Priorities Have Changed

As discussed in the previous chapter, police officers have placed the needs of their communities above their own for decades. This is about to change.

Officers have recently come under attack from the citizens they serve, their administration, and the government. It doesn't matter if the unrest is happening several thousand miles away. With today's media and social media, these incidents affect every city and police officer, regardless of the region in which they occur.

The reality is that these incidents are changing the mindset of the police. Officers are starting to do some soul searching of the direction they want their lives to go in. They are placing more priority on survival and retirement. They no longer feel the need to help everyone they serve. They no longer make the citizen's problem their problem. They no longer feel safe running into danger to help save a life. They are in preservation mode. It is becoming all about their families and themselves.

This brings something to mind: how many hard working Americans think about running into danger to help a fellow citizen? Not many. There are those few that will do what they can to help someone in need, but not at the cost of their lives or livelihood. Police officers are continually sent into harm's way, expected to resolve an issue or stop a violent offender. If they fail, they are crucified by the victims, the community, and most of all, by themselves.

So, as officers go to work every day, they talk more about family events and things they have done while off duty. Although this is extremely refreshing, it is not how it used to be. They used to discuss a problem residence or a problem neighborhood. They tried to figure out how to help someone through a difficult situation. Officers relied on their fellow officers for advice and support; however, this is diminishing quickly.

Officers still want to come in and serve their communities, but they are picking their battles more wisely. Officers aren't being as proactive as they used to be. They will patrol their beat areas as required, but they're not driving slowly with their heads on a swivel trying to catch the suspicious person crawling over your wall after just stealing property you worked hard for. Can you blame them?

God forbid they try to stop that suspicious person and that person tries to flee, or worse yet, turn and fight. They ask themselves "now what?" Is your property worth my family's financial security and anonymity? Unfortunately, no it's not. Officers would rather respond after the fact and take a crime report, possibly dust for fingerprints, so you can file a claim with your insurance carrier. Then, hopefully, the fingerprints will be traced back to a suspect and the officer will write an arrest warrant. If the warrant gets approved by a judge, then one day the suspect will get picked up. If that suspect fights, then it will be someone else's problem.

Officers would rather take hours of reports than risk their futures by fighting with a suspect with the possibility of being brought up on charges. I mean, there is no law requiring that an officer physically fight a suspect. So why do it? Officers' mindsets are moving away from protecting your property or family and are becoming more focused on protecting their own. Let it be known that police officers want to be out there fighting the good fight, even if they must risk their lives. It takes a great deal of restraint to change their mindset to being less proactive and more reactive. They want to stop the crime before it occurs; they want to catch the suspect crawling over your wall with your property so that justice can be served on your behalf. But they are beginning to rethink this, and the public better be prepared. For when the police stand down, the public better stand up.

Police officers are leaning towards helping the citizens they serve in order to learn how to better protect themselves. They will stay on a call for assistance a little while longer, trying to explain different ways in which the citizen can protect their property and family. Officers are aware of what's inevitably coming down the pipe. But, they want to make sure that those they serve are prepared. If you are reading this book and have had to call for police assistance, think about how long that responding officer stayed at your residence. Did they speak with you about ways to protect your property or about how to make the area around your house more secure? I'll bet they did. Some may argue that this is the function of the police. It is, in a way. Officers say it is a safe way to try to prepare the citizens to protect themselves, knowing that police response may be delayed.

In a lot of officers' minds is the idea that it is safer for them to arrive at the scene after the fact. This way, the possibility that they will have to use force upon a suspect or offender is reduced. Doing the paperwork is the safer alternative. As officers become more reluctant to use force upon a citizen, it becomes less likely that the offender will be caught—at least in the short term.

It is becoming less likely that police officers will take a risk with their careers or futures, or that of their families, by using force to affect an arrest. After all, the only requirements for police officers are to investigate crimes, to attempt to identify suspects, and to file criminal reports. There is no requirement to be proactive and to put yourself in a life-threatening situation.

Chapter 3: Depolicing

So, as I have previously mentioned in this book, depolicing is a rather new term within social reports and media outlets. Before we go into what depolicing is, let's visit what causes depolicing.

First of all, we need to understand that competition is a natural part of human behavior. People learn to be competitive during their early childhood years. This competitiveness grows as they mature and become adults. No one likes to lose. I have been a coach for several seasons for my daughter's soccer team. The main goal of the league that my daughter plays in is that the girls have FUN. As a coach, I always try to make sure that the girls have fun. But as they grow older, having fun is not why they show up week after week. They love to compete, and even more, they love to win! At the end of every game, the girls will run off the field and ask me, "Did we win?" Thankfully, this season we won—and won a lot!

You may be asking yourself, "What is he trying to say?" Well, you see, police officers are in constant competition with those committing crimes and trying to outsmart them. Police officers are competitive by nature. They are team players and love being part of a team with the same goal in mind: to serve and protect. But this hasn't been easy. Unfortunately, police officers very rarely win. A police officer will spend a lot of time trying to figure out crime trends within the areas they patrol, always trying to outsmart those committing the crimes.

The most rewarding thing is when an officer establishes probable cause to make an arrest of someone who has committed a crime against another citizen. The officer takes the offender into custody and transports them to jail. Later, the officer finds out that the case has been plead down to a lesser charge and that the offender is out of jail. For a short period of time, the officer sees a decrease in crime in the area where he or she has arrested the offender. The officer gets a feeling of accomplishment and pats himself on the back, since no one else will.

So, after a few weeks of diminished crimes in his area, he starts to see the same crimes being reported with the same MO of the suspect he had arrested just a few short weeks prior. The officer believes, a hunch, that it is the same offender that he had arrested previously. So now, the officer rolls slowly through the same neighborhood as where he last observed the offender. Low and behold, the officer sees the same offender walking in a neighborhood in which he doesn't live. So, this proactive officer stops the offender and tries to ascertain where he is going and why he is in the area. Let's imagine that the offender allows the officer to search his person. The officer finds evidence of a crime that he took a report for a few days earlier, so he places the same offender under arrest for the same crime. Then, again after a few short weeks, the case is plead down to a lesser offense, and the offender is again on the street ready to commit more crimes. This cycle repeats itself over and over, day after day, week after week. Do you think that that officer feels like he has accomplished his goal of removing a repeat offender off of the street? No.

You see, this cycle repeats itself for the full career of a police officer who works to keep his community safe. It is a thankless job in which you never really feel like you have accomplished anything. Every day, you get off of work feeling like you lost. If you take one drug dealer off of the street, there is another ready to take their place.

So, now we move into the modern day movement of not supporting the police. This topic is too in depth to cover in this short book. It has many facets that carry many different opinions. Remember, this book is written from the perspective of a police officer.

Like anything in life, things can go wrong. It happens daily in just about every field that entails human interaction. Words are misunderstood, people have bad days, and not everyone gets along. But in police work, if you have a bad day, or someone misunderstands your words, or you don't get along with a citizen, then your world can come crashing down in an instant. It is human nature to avoid confrontation. But when you face confrontation every day, you can't avoid it. The citizens expect you not to avoid it. They call the police when they are confronted. But who do the police call?

When confrontation comes looking for the police, they must react. If they run the other way, they can be brought up on charges of cowardice. That's very real. So when the police are confronted with confrontation, which is usually brought on with force or violence, who do they call when they are the only ones who can deal with it? There is no one the police can call when the "Thin Blue Line" is compromised. They must act.

When a police officer responds to confrontation, they must end it swiftly. If they don't, then the confrontation will keep coming. Police are not trained to retreat. When the police start retreating, society is in deep trouble. What then, call in the National Guard? Who do you think is coming if there is someone shooting people in a mall or a school? The police. Even if terror strikes us on our turf, do you think the military is going to come and take care of it? Nope. It is your neighborhood police officer. But what if they decide that it is no longer their top priority and that getting home safe is a better option? The officer would rather go home to their family than protect you from someone who is intent on killing as many people as possible with no regard for their own life.

So how does this relate to depolicing? There are many things that cause police officers to stand down. They can stem from issues ranging from the administration to fear. Yes, police officers, just like the general public, can become afraid. They just react to it differently. In cases in which police officers stand down due to administration issues, officers will temporarily shut down and "keep their heads down." This is short-lived, as the calls for service build up and they become engulfed in the calls they respond to. In most cases these officers will vent to their fellow squad mates, and after getting things off their chest, the ill feelings will subside and no longer bother them.

But when a police officer, or the law enforcement career, is scrutinized by the very public they are dedicated to protect, those ill feelings run deep and can become permanent. When an officer feels as though the whole world is against them, they tend to react as anyone else generally would. To better understand what I am talking about, I'd like to use an analogy that may seem trivial to some.

Let's look at how a dog learns how to act in response to its master's commands. There are two ways in which masters can teach their dogs how to behave. One of the techniques used is reward. Masters will reward their dog for good behavior. This reward teaches the dog to respond in a positive way.

This can usually be accomplished by anyone, not just the master. Once the dog is rewarded, he sees you as a friend and will dedicate himself to you.

The second technique is discipline. If a master uses a physical or a negative response to a certain behavior, the dog will start off obeying since they do not want to get struck. But after some time, the dog will see no benefit to obeying the master's commands and will shut down. They will refuse to come to the master for fear of being reprimanded. They will become isolated and antisocial. Sooner or later, this type of technique will have a negative effect on the relationship between the master and the dog. This type of behavior is usually resolved by putting the dog down.

How does this relate to the topic of depolicing? Although we are talking about two completely different types of beings, the behavior is parallel. Officers want only the best outcome for everyone they come into contact with throughout their shift. If they are dealing with a suspect, they want to take the suspect into custody and transport them to the magistrate without incident. The last thing a police officer wants to do is fight with a suspect, for the potential of injury is much too high.

As I discussed earlier, when a police officer uses force against a citizen, it will always have a shock and awe effect. Officers are trained to use a level of force that is a step above the force being used against them. So, of course, it will look like the officer is defeating the citizen. That's the goal, to end the conflict swiftly. But with the majority of the citizens in America having a source to videotape the actions of the police, the actions will be relived every time the video is viewed. You can pause it, view it in slow motion, and even take a still photo of the portion that is most interesting to you.

Police officers do not have the ability to predict what a suspect will do. They have to react to the situation that is unfolding in front of them. Pausing or delaying can have devastating consequences. So, how do officers protect themselves from public scrutiny? They don't put themselves in the public eye. They refrain from putting themselves in the position of having to use force. Since any call a police officer goes on presents them with the possibility of having to use force, they don't respond or wait until the situation settles down and then mop up the pieces.

When officers decide to put themselves in a position where their actions may be scrutinized or relived for weeks or months, by people who have never dealt with a violent situation or by those who avoid confrontation, they don't respond. One of the best things that was told to me as a young officer just starting out was "You can't control what people do or say, but you can control the way you react to it." Or maybe just don't react to it.

So with all of the negative attacks against the police that are going on today, more and more police officers across America just won't react to to the calls they receive. Response times will be delayed. Crime will increase, as is happening right now. No one will be held accountable for their actions against a fellow citizen. Police will view it as not worth losing their career, their reputation, or their freedom for. After all, it really isn't their problem. The problem was created long before the police responded.

To sum up this paragraph, the definition of depolicing is quite simple. Depolicing is when the police don't respond, or respond after the fact. Depolicing is when criminals increase their level of crimes or violence knowing that the police will not arrive to catch them. Depolicing is when the risk to police officers outweighs the reward. It is when police are not rewarded for their heroic actions but scrutinized for the actions they took. Depolicing is when the police are no longer proactive, no longer looking for crimes in progress, no longer looking for violent criminals, no longer willing to risk it all, so the citizens can feel safe in their homes.

Chapter 4: Is Society Ready to Protect Themselves?

So, if the way of the future is that communities across this great country will experience depolicing, are they ready to protect themselves? Probably not. As I discussed earlier, it is human nature to avoid conflict. But citizens don't call the police unless there is some type of confrontation. Citizens will no longer be able to avoid confrontation and will have to go against human nature.

It has been my experience that the police get calls for service from everything from violent crimes to child discipline. Yes, the police get called because Johnny won't get in the car to go to school. Johnny is ten and calling his mother names and being disrespectful. The police get these calls every hour of every day. The funny thing is the parent caller expects the police to do something about it. Some of them ask the officer to "light a fire under his butt!" So how does this affect the child's opinion of the police? It festers hatred and an anti-police belief.

So if some, and it is a rather low number, of the citizens can't control their own household, how are they going to control confrontation? That's a good question. They probably will not handle it very well. They will digress into the effect of human nature and avoid the confrontation. This will cause crime to skyrocket, and more and more people will lose property—or worse, their lives.

There are many ways citizens can learn to protect themselves. You can install lighting around your house. You can install surveillance cameras. You could purchase a firearm and be trained how to operate one. You could get a guard dog. This is just a short list.

Regardless of what you do to protect yourself or your property, it is inevitable that at some point you will need to call the police. For property issues, your insurance company will probably require you to file a report in order to receive compensation. The police will gladly respond to take that report for you. But if you are in a confrontation, you will have two options: fight or flight.

If depolicing becomes a reality, you may have to fight for your life or that of a family member. The police are coming, but it may be awhile. Once they arrive they may be hesitant to get in the fight with you. After all, your problem is not their problem. They will take the offender into custody, but they may not fight with them. The better option for the police may be to try and get an arrest warrant approved by a judge. Then, after several months, the offender will be arrested.

Your other option—the one probably most taken—is flight. You could always run the other way. Retreat! As a citizen you have a right to do this. The police officer doesn't. This may also be the safer option. Reduce your risk of injury, permanent injury, or death. This may sound cowardly to some, but as a citizen it isn't looked at as weakness. The police officer doesn't have this option. They can face an internal investigation and be brought up on a policy violation. Even lose their jobs.

As you can see, when the police arrive to your call for service they don't have the same options as you, the citizens, do. They must take actions, or the administration and the public will hold them accountable. Although the police are required to respond, there is no requirement on how fast they respond.

The point of this paragraph is to point out the fact that the public, in general, is not prepared to protect themselves. If the public isn't supporting the police then, quite possibly, the police won't support the public. If you don't believe this is true, then go on a ride along and see how the public responds to confrontation. I guarantee it will be an eye-opening experience.

Chapter 5: Where Do We Go from Here?

If you have made it to this point in the book, then you are probably asking yourself, "Where do we go from here?"

This is the million dollar question. As a current police officer, I can tell you that the condemnation of the police that occurs today is making a mark. Police officers hear it loud and clear. I am not going to get into my opinion of the ones speaking out loudly about police conduct. But the adage "walk a mile in my shoes" comes to mind. Generally, the street cop feels isolated and defeated.

If you recall, earlier in this book I used the analogy of the master and their dog. The first thing you could do in your community is let those officers that keep your streets safe and criminal-free know that you are thinking about them. This may fall on deaf ears at the start. Police fear getting baited into something that will come out later and damage their careers and reputations. But persistence pays off. Keep letting them know that you appreciate what they are doing and the sacrifices they are making for you and your family. Send letters of encouragement to the department to be posted or read during a pre-shift briefing. I can tell you that most of the officers will keep their heads in their computers, but they are listening. Just don't send doughnuts. Most modern-day police officers don't eat them.

The next thing you can do is reach out to the families of police officers. But don't just show up at the house without announcing your arrival. Officers have become very protective of their homes and families. Remember, their families are becoming—if not already—their top priority. If you know the spouse of a police officer, let them know how appreciative you are of their spouse's sacrifices and the dangers they put themselves in to keep you safe. The spouse of a police officer has a great amount of stress trying to keep their officer's mind in the game. Their fears of receiving the call that their husband, wife, son, or daughter will not be coming home again, ever, is a constant thought in their minds.

If you are computer savvy, start a blog or a community group to support those who will be the first to arrive if you're in trouble. Most officers don't read comments placed on news media outlets. Most of them are negative, so don't expect the officers to see them. With any luck, your post or blog will go viral and end up on one of the media outlets. Police do watch the news. It is required for officers to be up-to-date on local news.

Lastly, and probably the most aggressive option, is to attend a rally or protest and support the police. Now, this is probably the most dangerous. If this is a step you are willing to take to support those who would risk everything for you, be prepared to be outnumbered. With so many attendees of these rallies just wanting to be a part of something, the easiest target is the police. There is no regard for safety or sanity. The goal is to make as much noise and damage as possible to keep it in the news and relevant.

The only way to suppress the growing issue of depolicing in America is to make sure the police know that they are supported. Make them feel appreciated, and let them know that what they are doing is good. Help them help you by giving them the belief that no matter the outcome of their good-hearted decision, the citizens of the communities they protect will protect them.

Unfortunately, it will take a lot of work to reverse the depolicing mentality that has gripped law enforcement across the U.S. It really doesn't matter where the action or civil unrest occurred; police officers across this nation still will feel the effects. Just like anyone who hears of an incident in which something bad has happened to someone else, they tend to try to relate the circumstance to their own life. What would they do if that happened to them? It is no different for police officers who weren't involved in the incident that has created the civil unrest. Officers will inevitably place themselves in those officers' shoes. Unless there is a huge amount of support and reassurance from the community, sooner or later, those officers will stand down.

In order to move forward, we need to really support those putting their lives on the line. It needs to be an overwhelming response that is echoed nationwide. It must remove all doubt from the minds of police officers working in every community. The praise must ring out so loudly that it drowns out the negativity that is being spread throughout the media and social outlets. Most of all, it must be genuine—not meant to fulfill some type of propaganda or to gain support to win an election or reward.

Chapter 6: End of Watch

The murder rate for police officers across this country has accelerated beyond anything we have ever seen. Police officers are being executed, assaulted, and degraded every day. If they can't kill an officer outright, they will kill their spirit. This is a very slow death that has gripped many police officers. You feel like the world is against you, and you can do nothing right.

In my many years of experience in watching officers go from being the ambitious, new recruit ready to go save the world to the officer who is riding out the remaining year or two of their career, one thing I can say with complete certainty is that you can't just learn to be a police officer—it is something that is in your DNA. Of course, science will never find a special "gene" that identifies those who have it or don't.

Regardless of how unapproachable police officers may seem, they are still human. They do the best with what they have and have been trained in. Society is a never-ending evolving phenomenon that you cannot place a label on. Each call cannot be handled in the same manner, as each person is different from the next. You cannot train for every situation you will deal with as a police officer. No two domestic batteries are the same, no juvenile problem is the same, and no murder is the same. So, the police are left with doing what they believe is right for the situation they are confronted with. There is no amount of training you can give to a police officer that will fit every situation. When the Monday morning quarterbacks pick apart the actions of an officer, they are essentially destroying their motivation to respond.

As more and more youth move towards the side of the anti-police activists, the less people are available to carry the torch into the future. Young people are very influential and will go with whatever is popular. So, these young people will not see law enforcement as a means to make a living, creating a shortage of people to enter into this amazing career. The pool of candidates will drop off, and there will be a shortage of police officers.

Then, there are those who remain vigilant with their desire to help their community and hold the line between good and evil. But, how can they not second-guess whether or not they want to put themselves in a position that may destroy their futures due to their well-hearted actions? People don't like to be questioned—especially when they truly feel that their actions were appropriate given the situation; only to be disappointed time after time. Sooner or later they just won't make any more decisions, believing that regardless of whether or not the decision is right, someone will think it is wrong.

There are several ways to destroy police officers, aside from ending their lives. It starts by destroying their motivation and their belief that what they are doing is good. As the ridicule continues, it chips away at the officers' motivation to fight crime. They become isolated in their own minds and believe everyone is against them. They no longer look forward to starting their shifts and getting out on the street to do everything they can to help someone else.

As the screams of perceived bad decisions echo throughout the country, officers will become less proactive. They will respond to only those calls that come over their computers. The silent dispatches as they are called. Day after day, this runs through their minds. In their minds they figure "what's the point?" Officers will spend less time driving through neighborhoods to keep their presence known. They will avoid confrontation.

When a police officer avoids confrontation, as is human nature, the spirit of law enforcement dies. There is no memorial or bagpipes playing. There is no folding of the flag or a 21-gun salute. Thankfully, I guess, there is no funeral. It is not the end of watch for a police officer but the end of watch for protecting and serving.

When the concept of protecting and serving has died, then chaos will set in—maybe not immediately, but slowly. Surprised? You shouldn't be. What did you think would happen when you remove the only wall between order and chaos? Who knows? Maybe this is what needs to happen in order for citizens to realize how important the police are. When this becomes a popular mindset for the majority of police officers, everyone is in trouble.

Realize this: the statement "end of watch" doesn't need to identify a police officer's death. It could mean the end of the watchful eye of the police officers on the street all day and all night, trying to stop evil from entering your world—and from destroying your life. They'll be there without hesitation, sacrificing their lives for yours. For now.

Chapter 7: Smile, You're on Camera

Over the last several years, the issues of police camera have become the subject of many "use of force" debates. Proponents of body cameras have said that the use of these cameras will hold the officers accountable and reveal the true details of when police use force and if the force is justified. Opponents of the use of body cameras have held that it is an invasion of privacy for the police officers, as body cameras have the high possibility of recording officers while they are engaged in private calls with their families or between themselves and other officers.

In my experience, the use of body cameras has not been accepted by officers around the country—whether or not they're concerned about the ramifications after the video is viewed or feel that they are being micromanaged. Administrators need to make sure that the policies and procedures enacted for the use of cameras clearly protect both the officer and the citizen.

In the beginning, administrators tried to "sell" the use of cameras to their officers by telling them it would reduce the amount of time the officer would spend in court because the incident, or confession, would be caught on audio and video. When you can keep an officer from having to appear in court, you will immediately get their attention.

It has been my experience that this is not the case. On several occasions, I have heard from officers that there are times when the attorneys do not introduce or even view the video. Now, being that this is what some administrators have used to get the officer to accept the use of video cameras, then when it appears not to be the case, officers feel betrayed. Once an officer feels betrayed, you may never get them to trust you again.

The other issue that has caused extreme distrust of the use of cameras is that officers fear nothing more than being put on notice that they are being investigated by IA, or Internal Affairs. This fear manifests itself into a "stand down" mentality. Once an officer is put on notice, you can bet that their motivation to be proactive quickly diminishes. This usually holds true until after the results of the investigation are known. If the officer is found to be exonerated, then they will go back to being proactive and after a few weeks of cooling off, an officer will perform as they always did.

So, why would the officer not want an audio or video recording of the incident that shows that they did everything right? This has nothing to do with the incident. Let me break it down for you. If a citizen files a complaint against an officer, it will more than likely end up in IA. The days of complaints being handled at the supervisor level are vanishing. Departments are sending more complaints directly to IA, even minor "he cussed at me" complaints.

So, IA receives the complaint, and the first thing the investigator does is pull the video. After reviewing the video, the officer may be exonerated of the complaint, and the investigator will close the case as unfounded. Here's the hook. If, while reviewing the video, the investigator sees a policy violation unrelated to the complaint, the investigator will open a new case against the officer for the policy violation. This could be as minor as not wearing your reflective vest at an accident scene. Since it is clear in the video, you are found guilty and reprimanded. You may receive a letter in your personnel file—or even be terminated.

For those officers looking to go on to be a detective or be promoted, this small violation can wreak havoc on that office's ability to move on. Some departments will not allow you to apply to move to a "specialized unit" or be promoted if you have had a letter in your file the year prior to applying. Policy and procedure is a double-edged sword. At times you have to violate one policy to adhere to another. So you are left to pick your poison.

I think, for the most part, officers are becoming more comfortable with the use of cameras. They know that they are not going away and are seeing that they have been exonerated on complaints and have come to accept it. But there is no doubt that it has changed how police do their jobs—and not all of this change is good.

I was talking with a group of officers, and one of them brought up a good question: why have videos of officers using force become so mainstream? It stopped me in my tracks. I guess I can understand why, but why not?

The thoughts of officers may be why only show the officers and not show how the officer is treated at a scene. When we walk into a residence and are bombarded by curse words and screaming. This is always shocking. "You called us!" We're here because someone thought something was going wrong and the police were needed. So why not show what goes on inside of "your" house? You see me for 10 hours of video a day.

I think, for obvious reasons, administrators will only show the media requests. The Fair Information Act requires releasing the information upon request. Do you think videos of people threatening the police or degrading them with curse words and derogatory comments will somehow make the news? Many officers believe that if these videos were released, the public may rethink their support for police body cameras.

Police departments across America are not willing to compete to determine whose video is better than whose. It cannot become some type of social competition and will not do anything for the relationship between departments and the citizens they serve.

Another area needs to be closely looked at when demanding that police agencies purchase and maintain a quality mobile audio and video system. With so many municipalities struggling with mounting debt, adding police cameras will only hamper the departments' ability to add police officers to the streets.

As the government pushes to require that every officer wear a body camera, the cost cannot be ignored. I cannot provide you with facts pertaining to the cost of these camera systems. That is research you can do on your own, as police budgets are public information. But I can give you an idea of how it can affect budgets.

So, the federal government hands out grants to agencies to purchase cameras for each police officer and patrol car in their department. Each patrol car usually has two cameras: one on the front windshield and the other pointing to the backseat. This usually includes a certain amount of memory to hold onto the videos that are uploaded from each of the cameras. Agencies will put in place policies that will determine how long the video is stored. Things like arrests and use of force videos will be retained for much longer than just routine citizen contacts. This grant is usually used to cover as many cameras that the department has on staff at the time the grant is issued.

What many departments are discovering is that the initial memory that is included in the initial purchase is not enough to store thousands of hours of video. If you research the statistics of how many contacts police officers have each year you will be amazed. There are millions of contacts between citizens and police each year. Now, let's say the contact lasts for an hour. As determined through Terry v. Ohio, a police contact can last up to an hour before the person must be arrested or released. So, let's say the contact lasts for forty-five minutes. After that time, the officer establishes probable cause to arrest the person. The officer then completes the paperwork while still on scene before transporting the person to jail. Those types of contacts could take up to two hours, depending on the crime.

Once the officer arrives at the jail, he turns off the video and "tags" the video usually with a report number and the person's name. It then stays on the on board DVR until the end of the shift. The officer then completes the remaining paperwork and leaves the jail. They then return to their patrol duties.

At the end of the officer's shift, they return to their substation and the video is automatically uploaded to the department database where it is stored. The video is then tagged with the type of recording it is—arrest, use of force, or citizen contact. It will stay there for the determined amount of time specified in policy. Some of the systems out there require the officer to actually manually upload his series of videos from his shift.

As you can imagine, this takes a lot of memory to store all of these contacts. So, agencies across the country are having to purchase more and more memory in order to have an adequate amount to be able to store these video files. This places an extreme burden on agencies to have to increase their budgets in order to maintain these systems. As far as I understand, the department I work with has had to purchase more memory twice since installing the cameras approximately four years ago. That is just for more memory space. Think about having to replace damaged or malfunctioning cameras? This is another huge expense that agencies have had to deal with. As you can see this, this can add up quickly and take away from hiring new officers to backfill retired positions and to expand the level of patrol officers on the street. With crime increasing, regardless of what you hear, the need for more police also increases. This puts departments in a very difficult position.

Administrations are having to cut budgets in areas that have proven to make a difference within the community in order to maintain these camera systems. As I'm sure you are aware, technology fails often. You can bet that when an officer is involved in a physical confrontation, it's very likely that his body camera will get damaged. Computers crash, and software needs updates frequently. The unfortunate aspect of this is that in most departments with camera systems, the officer is held responsible. You better know if your camera is working because if it's not, you'll violate the policy and can be reprimanded, suspended, or terminated.

The other aspect of camera systems is that most of them will only record if you're within a certain distance of your patrol vehicle. The camera systems that my department uses have a distance of 12-1,500 feet. This means that if you are outside of that distance, your audio recording will not work. You guessed it: you can be held responsible if your recorder doesn't record your contact. So, as you can see, there are some very real reasons why some officers are against the use of cameras. There are too many variables in place that can "hem you up" even if your intentions were good.

Chapter 8: Final Call

So, I have discussed some very real and factual concerns of the effects of depolicing. We have discussed the police mindset and how it can affect how police respond to calls for service and how your problem will no longer be their problem. Police officers will change their priorities, which will change the landscape of policing. Reward over reprimand is what every human being searches for. If you praise and respect people, they will inevitably do great things. But if you continue to punish and degrade them, they will no longer respond—not mentally, anyway.

Depolicing is a very real and scary phenomenon that is taking hold across the country. Society will either have to fight or flee because you'll be left fighting your own battles. In most cases, they put themselves in these battles and want someone to help them out. Calls for service will never go unanswered, but they will be delayed. Police officers will no longer have the competitive edge they once had. They will "play it safe" and choose their battles more wisely. Officers will decide that taking a report and writing a warrant is the wiser choice. When the criminal element figures this out, the crime rates will spike and remain high.

Officers feel defeated day in, day out. They feel as though no one is on their side. Feelings of putting their lives, careers, and families on the line are beginning to take hold. After all, no one cares, and no one is standing up for them. We've discussed what it will take for these feelings of despair to fall away and what the police supporters can do to make a difference in a police officer's life. We've discussed how to show those walking the line that their work is not for nothing—it's the only thing between calm and chaos.

We have shown that police use of force has a shock and awe effect when viewed from the inexperienced eye. Those who dissect what the police have done have never walked into a dark building looking for a suspect who might be armed. They've never pulled a domestic batterer off of their victim to stop an evil assault. Those unexperienced eyes have never had to talk down a suicidal subject who had a gun to their head with their finger on the trigger. They haven't talked endlessly to the same person who then decides to pull the trigger—only to have to go back to the station to change their uniform because they were covered in blood from the person who just put a bullet through their head while standing 30 feet in front of them. Then go back in service to handle Johnny, who's disrespecting his parent's calls.

Sooner or later, the citizens are going to have to learn to protect themselves. They're going to have to learn to either accept what's happening to them or stop the threat in front of them. It is a very cold world out there, and the police have given the people some warmth, some hope that tomorrow will be okay. The police are here to stay. They will go out there day in, day out. But, if the passion of proactive policing goes away, the only concept left is reactionary policing.

I don't want you to get the wrong idea. The fire to protect those who can't protect themselves will still burn deep within the souls of the police officers working in your communities. But it is smoldered by the degrading, disrespectful, and untrained actions of those around you. As with any fire, no matter how low the fire burns, it will only take a small amount of kindling to reignite that fire. The police are going to be there. It's in their DNA. But their fight and purpose is getting weaker.

www.ingramcontent.com/pod-product-compliance
Lightning Source LLC
Chambersburg PA
CBHW071020290526
45795CB00005B/1881